LILLENAS DRAMA

DRAMA NOW!

A DRAMA WORKSHOP TO JUMP-START MINISTRY

BY CHUCK NEIGHBORS

Lillenas® PUBLISHING COMPANY
KANSAS CITY, MO 64141

Printed in the United States.

Questions? Please write or call:
Lillenas Publishing Company
Drama Resources
P.O. Box 419527
Kansas City, MO 64141
Phone: 816-931-1900 • Fax: 816-412-8390
E-mail: drama@lillenas.com
Web site: www.lillenasdrama.com

Cover art by Brandon Hill

Contents

CHAPTER 1

Why Am I Doing This?

Since 1975 I have made a career of performing and teaching drama geared to the local church. Drama has experienced a rebirth in the life of the church and it is an exciting time to be a Christian involved in theatre arts! Church-based drama ministries are thriving and the quality of theatre being produced is rising. All good stuff!

But there is a problem. While a few churches have qualified directors and individuals with theatre experience, many do not; and those who do have training are usually only a fraction of those on the drama team.

One of the questions that I am asked most frequently is, "How do we get started?" My answer is always, "You need to hold a drama workshop."

Ideally, you would hire a professional to come in and conduct the workshop for you. Indeed, that has been one of the things I have enjoyed doing for countless churches around the country. It is a great idea to have a guest instructor conduct the workshop—even if you already have a qualified director/teacher in your midst. Why? In a word—reinforcement. Almost without fail, every time I conduct a workshop the church drama director affirms that one of the best things to come out of the workshop is the fact that having me teach has given credibility to the things they have been teaching. They say, "Now they will believe me when I tell them they have to turn toward the audience or project their voice more," etc. This, and the fact that the team is being trained at all, is a great reason to have someone from the outside conduct the workshop.

But what if you can't afford someone else or don't know who to get in your area? This is the reason for this resource. I believe that if you have a little bit of experience as a performer or actor, and perhaps have taken a drama class or two, you can conduct this workshop yourself. And please note, while this book is written primarily for directors of church drama ministries, it can also serve as a good hands-on resource for the actor, serving to reinforce and remind individual performers of the basics of acting.

You'll find that this workshop practically teaches itself. Your role is more of a facilitator than that of a teacher (although there are a few places that you will have to play the role of teacher). The workshop is participatory with a "learn-by-doing" approach. It is exercise-driven and most of the "teaching" is done in the discussions following the exercises. I have strived to make the exercises as simple to follow as possible. Each exercise will contain:

PURPOSE—makes it clear why you are doing this activity.

DO THIS—instructions to you, the facilitator, in setting up the exercise.

DEBRIEF

A time to stop, gather with your actors and talk about what you've just done; share insights and applications; and how they could improve on the skills highlighted in the exercise.

SAY THIS—gives you a sample of how to give instructions for the exercise.

⌘ ***Side Coach***—*if applicable, for instructions and tips to give out while the exercise is being done.*

The workshop accomplishes several things:

- It will serve as basic training for your actors. Even if you have team members with previous experience in theatre, the workshop will serve to get everybody on the same page in terms of structure, vocabulary, and procedures.
- The workshop gives you an opportunity to establish the rules of the stage and rehearsal, as well as define the roles of the actor and the director.
- This is also a great time to scope the talent in your group. It will serve as an informal audition.
- Finally, the experience will serve as a team-building exercise. The very experience of being together for a day of intense activity will accomplish much in unifying your team and building trust among the members.

The whole event is meant to be fun, interactive, and a time of discovery for you and your team.

CHAPTER 2

Getting Started

This workshop is designed as a day-long event and should be able to fit nicely into a six-hour block with a break in the middle for lunch. Alternately, you could offer it as a course over several nights; however, if you do, I would strongly suggest that they be successive nights rather than one night a week. You'll find that the team members will retain the training better if it is more intensive. One of the major benefits of the workshop model is the community that is built over the time spent together, which is much easier to achieve in the one-day model.

Since we want to build community among team members, be sure to allow time for informal visiting. This happens well over food and beverage. Setting up a continental breakfast is a great way to set the tone. Be sure to provide name tags if there will be people present who do not know the rest of the participants.

The day could look something like this:

8:45 A.M.	Continental breakfast
9:00	Session begins
Noon	Break for lunch
1:00 P.M.	Session resumes
4:00	The end

Introduction

Give the group a brief overview of the day, but avoid talking too long here. Set the tone for the day by *doing* something. A good mixer is a great way to start. Keep in mind that every exercise will have a purpose. Here is a good mixer to start off the session:

Mingle Mosey

PURPOSE: To mix up the group, allowing them to meet others. Begin breaking down inhibitions. Getting to know others.

DO THIS: Divide the room into two equal groups.

SAY THIS: The group on the right side of the room is now the "Mingle Family." Your names are now your real first names combined with your new last name, Mingle. The same instruction goes for the other half of the room, the "Mosey Family." Now the Mingles are going to meet the Moseys. I want you to mill around the room and introduce yourselves to as many people as possible. Af-

ter awhile I will yell, "stop" (or "freeze"); at that time the person you are greeting will become your partner. If for some reason you do not have a partner, raise your hand and look for someone else with their hand raised and partner with that person. (If the number does not come out evenly you can form a group of three or you could put yourself in the exercise to make it work.)

Tip: This is a good time to explain a rule that you will use throughout the day. Since there will be lots of interactive activity going on all day, you'll want to establish a method of getting everybody quiet without screaming at them—to save your voice. This is a method you may have learned in kindergarten but it is still effective with adults. Instruct the group that if you need them to quiet down you will simply raise your hand. If they see your hand raised, they are to close their mouths and raise their hands. If everyone follows instructions, you'll find the room gets quiet fairly quickly. Rehearse this once with the group.

DO THIS: Give them some time to "mingle mosey" and then stop and have them partner up. Once everyone has a partner, you give them an assignment. Remember, these assignments will have an application to drama, but we will get to that later.

First Assignment: Fret and Fuss

SAY THIS: I want you to think of something that irritates you: a pet peeve or something that makes you upset or angry. Now I want you to share that with your partner for one minute (time them). Begin.

(You will notice most people will simply be telling their partner about the thing that upsets them. This is not the goal. You want them to feel that emotion—this is acting, after all! Stop them and renew the instruction.)

Stop! Hold it! I think you misunderstood. I want you to really get into it. Red faces, angry gestures, wild emotion! And remember that people who are upset are not very good listeners. Don't listen to your partner—both of you fret and fuss at the same time. Now, try it again.

DO THIS: After the minute is up, stop the group and perhaps give a little commentary about communication: "We are not very good listeners when we are upset. Today is not only about drama but also understanding that good drama also mirrors real life aspects of communication."

Set them in motion with Mingle Mosey again and after a few moments stop and have them partner up again.

Second Assignment: Top Three List

SAY THIS: Now, I want each person to think of three things that they are most thankful for. You again have one minute to share those things with your partner (you don't really have to keep time on this one). This time I really do want you to listen to what your partner has to say.

DO THIS: Let them share the information. After they have gone for a minute or so, stop them. Take a moment to point out the difference in the sound of the room as compared to the Fret and Fuss exercise. Also, note the difference in how they were communicating with each other in contrast to Fret and Fuss.

Hopefully, you will notice a difference in the group at this time. The ice is broken and people are a bit more relaxed and comfortable. Have everyone take their seats and move on to the next step.

Discussion:

Why Are You Here?

Why Drama?

What Does It Take To Make It Work?

Why Are You Here?

Now you can move into a discussion time where you will establish the focus for the day. Depending on the size of the group, you might go around the room and have everyone introduce themselves and perhaps give a sentence or two about why they came to the workshop (love drama, looking for a place to serve, a friend twisted my arm). If the group is not too large, you could also mix in something interesting to help them get to know each other like "tell us a hobby or something that nobody else in the room knows about you." This gives you, the leader, a better understanding of just who you are working with.

Why Drama?

This is a very important discussion where you will explore the purpose of drama in the life of the church. Don't panic; you are likely to discover that the group will give you all the answers that you are looking for. I like to set up the discussion with this hypothetical situation:

You have just performed a play in the worship service and after the service, a person approaches you with these statements: "I don't think drama belongs in the church. I don't think the church should be a place of entertainment."

What would you say to that person? At the end of this book I have included several articles that will help answer the "Why drama?" question. I encourage you to read those articles in preparation for this discussion. But, in short, the answers you are looking for and are likely to hear from the group are (in no particular order):

- Cultural relevance.
- We remember and learn by seeing as well as hearing.
- We live in an entertainment-oriented culture and are accustomed to getting our information through the arts.
- We are a storied people and we learn through story.
- Jesus was a storyteller (parables) and plays are similar to parables.
- People identify with characters they see onstage, which makes for powerful communication.

- Provides a way for people to serve the church using their talents and gifts.
- While many may think this is a "new thing," drama began in the church and has a long history in religious context.

Feel free to expound on these observations. Having people own these reasons will help them understand and appreciate their talents and gifts as they relate to service in the church.

What Does It Take To Make It Work?

Here is a chance at the outset to help people identify some of the things that are going to be required in order to have a successful drama ministry. The goal is to help people realize that good drama ministries don't just happen. They take work, planning, and discipline. So again, in discussion mode, ask people to list what they think it is going to take. Here are some of the answers you are looking for (again, in no particular order):

- People
- Material (scripts)
- Rehearsal space
- Leadership/Director
- Commitment
- Costumes, sets, and props
- Technical support: lighting, sound, etc.
- Good communication between the drama team leader and the pastoral staff

That last one is huge, especially if your plan is to include drama on a regular basis in your worship services. At the end of the day or at your next meeting, you may want to craft a vision statement for your ministry. The two discussions you have just had will set up the foundation for that statement.

Tip: *A Special Guest!* This is a great time in the workshop to have a word of greeting and encouragement from the pastor and/or worship leader of your church. If possible, it would be excellent if they would participate in the whole day—just to get an understanding of what goes into making drama work, if for no other reason. But to at least show up and give a word of encouragement and endorsement will help elevate this in the minds of those attending. It makes the statement that "this is important to the life of our church." The pastor giving voice to the vision and mission of the church, and how drama is a part of that, will go a long way in validating your efforts!

Now, let the fun begin!

CHAPTER 3

Acting Basics—Inhibition

One of the first obstacles to getting started for beginning actors is fear. Fear of getting up onstage and making a fool out of themselves, fear of blowing their lines, fear of not being accepted by their fellow actors or by the audience. We need to tackle this fear head on. One of the best ways to do that is through games designed to break down inhibition. Acting involves taking risks, and before I can expect actors to take risks in front of an audience, they need to be comfortable taking them in front of the rest of the team. These exercises are designed to do just that. And remember, you can use these exercises not only for this workshop but for future rehearsal times as well.

Loosening Up and Stretching Exercises

PURPOSE: To loosen up the group, and their bodies, both at the same time. To get the actors in the mind-set that acting is a physical activity, not just a verbal one.

DO THIS: Have everyone stand in a large circle. Have them spread out so there is plenty of room between people.

SAY THIS: To get started, we need to understand that acting is a physical activity. We are going to spend much of our time today using our bodies, so we need to get them limbered up and ready to perform.

DO THIS: Lead the group in several stretching exercises. Stretch upward on tiptoes like they are going to touch the ceiling, then flop over like a rag doll, bending at the waist. Do this a couple of times. Now, from the rag doll position, have them stand up slowly as if they are a marionette being pulled upright by strings attached to various parts of the body.

Start everyone shaking their right hand. Then add their left hand. Now expand to shaking the whole arm and keep adding: the feet, the body, the head. Keep doing this and make a vocal sound at the same time.

Finally, do some isolation exercises. Have them drop their heads forward and then slowly roll the head around their shoulders, rolling to the left for a couple circles and then to the right. Next, do circles with the shoulders: first the right, then the left, then both at the same time. You could keep going: add the hips, bend and rotate from the waist, do the legs and the feet.

Copycat

PURPOSE: To break down inhibition and break the ice, get people comfortable doing things in front of each other.

DO THIS: Have everyone stand in a large circle. Have them spread out so there is plenty of room between people.

SAY THIS: I know you are all probably afraid that I am going to somehow make you look like a fool today. The fear of looking like a fool is very common among performers. One of the best ways to get over that fear is to make everyone look like a fool at the same time so nobody feels self-conscious about it. To do that, we are going to play a game called Copycat. The rules are quite simple. I am going to start by doing something crazy, like acting like an animal, making weird noises, silly movements—really anything that comes to mind. So that I don't feel foolish doing this, I want you to do exactly what I am doing at the same time—just like a copycat! After I have seen that everyone is copying me, I will point to someone else in the circle and they will do the first thing that pops into their head and we will all copy them. We will just keep tossing it around the room for awhile. Because we are all going to be doing this, the only people who should feel foolish are those who are not participating! Let's begin.

⌘ *Side Coach: Encourage people to do the first thing that comes to mind. Be spontaneous. Don't waste time "trying to think of something"—just do it! Encourage people to use sound and movement together. The more outlandish, the better.*

Yes, Let's!

PURPOSE: To break down inhibition. To encourage spontaneity and imagination.

DO THIS: Have the actors spread out over the room. They need to find some space that is not too close to someone else.

SAY THIS: Now we are going to use our imagination like when we were little children playing all by ourselves. For this game, it might help you to think of yourself as back in kindergarten. I am going to call out an activity like this: "Let's ride a bike." I want you to all answer back in unison, "Yes, let's!" Then I want you to go into your own little world and pretend you are riding a bike. Don't watch others, you don't have to interact with anyone else—it's just you riding a bike. Then after we have all done that for awhile, someone else in the room calls out a new activity and we all again respond in unison with, "Yes, let's!" and immediately pretend to do that activity. We will keep this going until we have done several different activities.

(Sample activities: brushing teeth, playing basketball, climbing a mountain, etc.)

⌘ *Side Coach: Don't watch everyone else—just do your own thing. Keep encouraging new activities after the group has done one for 10 seconds or so. Use the whole room —you don't have to stay in one spot.*

DEBRIEF

After you have done this series of exercises, it is time to talk about it. This is where the actors begin to see why we did what we did, and then learn from the experience. Encourage everyone to take a seat and ask the following questions for discussion:

Q: What was the purpose of those exercises?

Q: What has happened to the atmosphere in the room since doing those exercises?

Q: When we first started, if I was to ask somebody to act like, say, a monkey, I probably would not have gotten many volunteers. But now if I asked somebody, do you think people would be more likely to comply? Why?

CHAPTER 4

Acting Basics—Body Control

It may surprise you and your team, but we are going to spend quite a bit of our day focused on body control. Proportionately, probably about half of the workshop time will deal with the physical aspects of acting. Why? Acting is a visual medium. Our bodies are instruments to be used to communicate our message. Often what we say with our bodies is just as important as the lines we recite. Actors need to become aware of this and learn to use and train their bodies to say what we want them to say. The next group of exercises will help us grasp this concept.

The first thing we need to do is to get people in small groups of 4 or 5. You can do this in a number of ways, counting off or forming groups close to where they are sitting, but that is so mundane! Let's instead continue to reinforce the inhibition theme and group people with a game called . . .

Barnyard

PURPOSE: To divide people into groups in a way that helps breakdown inhibitions and also facilitates people working with others that they might not usually choose. Building community.

DO THIS: Figure out how many groups you will need in order to have 4 or 5 people in each group. Come up with the names of animals that correspond to that number of groups. For example, if you want 5 groups, then you could have: cow, horse, chicken, sheep, and pig.

SAY THIS: In order to put you into groups, I am going to come around, point at you, and call you the name of an animal. Remember the animal, but please don't take it personally (go around and assign the names). Now, making only the *sound* of your animal, find everybody that is the same animal as you.

DO THIS: Now that people are in groups, you need to spread the various groups out in the room so that they have some room to work independently of each other. You are now ready for the first group assignment.

▼ *Variation: You could do this exercise with songs, foreign accents or famous people impersonations.*

(Note: There will be several group assignments during the day. If the place you are meeting has adjoining classrooms, you may want to use them as an option for group assignments when they are preparing things to be performed throughout the day.)

Group Pantomimes

PURPOSE: To illustrate how we can communicate without words. To build teamwork in small groups.

Each group will be given an assignment to be performed as a group. Depending on the number of people and time constraints, you could have each group do every kind of pantomime, or to expedite things you can give each small group a different kind of pantomime. I usually end up doing the latter.

DO THIS: In advance, prepare some lists. I'll get you started, but you can easily customize this and create your own. The lists are:

- Household machines: sewing machine, toaster, washing machine, lawn mower, tape recorder
- Things that happen in nature: sunset, waterfall, tornado, leaves falling, flowers blooming
- Abstract machines: love, fear, prejudice, confusion, apathy

SAY THIS: I am going to come around to each group and give you an individual assignment. (Each group will have a different assignment, so do this secretly.) The idea is to work as a group to create a pantomime that communicates the thing assigned to your group. There is no talking or noises allowed in the performance of these pantomimes. You will need to work fast as you will only have about 3-5 minutes to prepare. After the time is up, we will all come together and perform the pantomimes for each other.

DO THIS: Go around to each group and assign the various things. Perhaps two groups perform household machines, two do things from nature, and two do abstract machines. The abstract machines take a little more explanation and are a bit more challenging. You might want to assign the abstract machines first in order to give those groups a bit more time. The abstract machines can be explained as machines designed to communicate the abstract ideas. They can resemble a familiar machine (car, assembly line, washing machine) or be unlike anything we have ever seen before. The main goal is to communicate the abstract only using our bodies. After you have assigned, allow them the time allotted to complete the task.

⌘ *Side Coach: Remember these performances are to be done silently in pantomime. You are to all be a part of the thing you are creating, NOT the person using or affected by the creation.*

After the time is up, you are ready for the first real performances of the day. Assemble the groups back together as an audience and perform the pantomimes for each other. The audience is encouraged to guess what each thing is, but make sure each group completes its pantomime rather than stopping because somebody guessed the right thing.

DEBRIEF

Some questions to discuss:

Q: What have you learned from this experience?

Q: How was it working with your group?

Q: What was the most challenging part of the exercise?

The things you want to emphasize are the ways that they communicated ideas without words, using only their bodies. Also, build in the idea of teamwork. They worked together to create these performances—they relied on one another to get the message across.

Tip: This first performance is a good place to teach a little audience etiquette—and church audiences need to be taught these things. Encourage applause at the end of the performance. Remind the different groups that this is not a time to continue fine-tuning their upcoming performance—no talking! They need to give the performers 100% of their attention.

Michelangelos

PURPOSE: To show how our bodies communicate messages. To encourage creative expression.

This is one of my favorite workshop exercises! I like it because it not only gives an opportunity to teach, but also because it is a concept that is easily adaptable into a performance piece. It is a tried and true technique that is used by many drama instructors. It also goes by the names of Potter and Clay, and Tableaus. The basic idea is to build sculptures or tableaus based on ideas that you give to the group.

DO THIS: Once again you will need a list, prepared in advance, of about five ideas to be turned into sculptures. Here are five suggestions, but feel free to create your own:

- Enthusiasm
- Prejudice
- "Do unto others as you would have them do unto you" (The Golden Rule)

- Scene from the story of the Prodigal Son
- What is Worship?

Instruct everyone to get back into their small groups from the pantomime.

SAY THIS: We are now going to do an exercise called Michelangelos. One person from each group will become "Michelangelo," a sculptor. The others in the group will become lumps of clay. Michelangelo will make a sculpture of an idea that I am going to give you using the "lumps of clay" to make his/her art. This is a non-verbal exercise, so no talking is allowed by either Michelangelo or the lumps of clay. You will only have one minute to make this sculpture, so think and work fast. Go from the first impulse that hits you—chances are that if you thought about it for five minutes you would do pretty much the same thing anyway. Each person will get a chance to do one of these, and they get harder as we go along . . . so who is going to be the first volunteer in your group (each group selects who in their group will go first)? OK, the first word I am going to give you is "enthusiasm." You have one minute. Go!

Tip: When explaining how the sculpture is done, use a volunteer as a lump of clay and demonstrate how you can sculpt them. Move their body into several poses. Show how you can create facial expressions, focus the eyes (by pointing where you want them focused), etc. This example will help people to get it very quickly. Also be aware and sensitive to the fact that this exercise requires a lot of physical touch, which brings in another aspect of inhibition.

⌘ *Side Coach: Remember—no talking! Don't tell them what to do—mold them. Lumps of clay, you need to concentrate. Try not to laugh. You have 30 seconds. You have 15 seconds. You have 5 seconds. Freeze!*

DO THIS: At the end of the minute, tell everyone (except the Michelangelo) to freeze. Then tell the Michelangelos to imagine that they are in a museum and to walk around and see what other people have created to communicate enthusiasm. Pick what you consider the best sculpture. After the Michelangelos have viewed all the sculptures, tell everyone to unfreeze (except the one group you have selected) and to come over and look at the one you have selected. Now, as a group, you are going to analyze this one sculpture.

SAY THIS: What is it about this sculpture that communicates the idea of enthusiasm?

As people discuss what they see, you will discover opportunities to share insight into how our bodies communicate. In order to sculpt "enthusiasm," we had to tap into what it looks and feels like; raised arms, smiles, cheers, big eyes, mouths open. All these things that are part of communicating one simple word have tremendous application to the acting process.

After you have identified as many things as you can, tell the actors to unfreeze.

You then move back to the groups to do the next sculpture, repeating the above instructions. Before each one begins, use each new sculpture to teach and add elements of good stage pictures. Things to include are:

- Establish a point of view. Where do people stand to view this art? Compare this to work onstage.
- Make sure everyone can be seen. Don't let people block (stand in front of others so they can't be seen by the audience) each other in the sculpture. Don't have people stand with their backs to the audience.
- Straight lines are boring. Make your art three-dimensional. Avoid placing people in straight lines; instead build triangles with the bodies onstage.
- Levels are interesting. Have some people sit, some stand, and some kneel for intriguing pictures.
- Include touch and eye contact with the individuals in the sculpture, if appropriate.
- When it comes to a story, think contrast and conflict. Everybody standing with their arms in the air does say "enthusiasm." We have a story though if we take one person out and make them sad. Now there is something happening that is interesting to watch rather than everybody doing the same thing.

DEBRIEF

Once again, we have used our bodies to get ideas across without spoken word. Ask these questions:

Q: What did you learn/observe from that exercise?

Q: Was it difficult to hold one position for a long period of time?

Q: As you created these scenes, where did the pictures you sculpted come from?

Additional things to layer into each new sculpture:

- For the "prejudice" sculpture think about contrast. This is a good one to show different attitudes and build the idea of a story.
- For the Golden Rule sculpture, encourage eye contact and touch.
- For the prodigal son scene, remind people that there are many scenes in this story (most people want to do the last scene). Encourage variety.

- For the worship sculpture, encourage people to think "big picture." Worship is more than just what happens on Sunday morning (Romans 12:1).

This is an exercise that can be easily turned into a performance! By simply memorizing a few positions in a tableau, you can create powerful images in front of an audience. Ask the group to brainstorm some ideas for using this. Some ideas I have used or heard of are:

- Sculptures based on scripture (a different picture for different verses or ideas). Try The Beatitudes, a parable (like the Prodigal Son) or the 23rd Psalm.
- Sculptures to a song that has strong imagery. Think in terms of "moving pictures."
- Sculptures that illustrate a sermon. An example might be a sermon on how we worship God in our daily lives. At various points in the sermon we could see a sculpture showing people in prayer, people serving others, people visiting the sick, etc.
- A fun teaching tool in the classroom. Children love to do this exercise and would enjoy it as a visual aid in teaching almost any story.

The point is to be creative and use this as a springboard for performance. This is also a good "first performance" for actors, as it can get them in front of any audience without the stress of memorizing lines.

CHAPTER 5

Acting Basics—Body Movement and the Stage

No, I am not being redundant here. Body control and body movement are two different things. Body control has to do with becoming aware of our body and how it can be used to communicate. Body movement has more to do with the rules of the stage. (Yes, there are rules!) This is where we will get into the proper way to stand, sit, and walk onstage. We will deal a bit with what to do with our hands, how to use props, and some other things that will help us look good in front of an audience. While a character we portray onstage can express a lot with posture and movement, too often we will look just like ourselves onstage rather than the character. It is best to start from a neutral position and way of movement, and then layer on the character rather than to fall into the trap of always moving the way we are used to in real life!

This section is going to be a brief overview that can fit nicely into our format of a one-day workshop. However, these "rules" need to become habits and that takes more practice and time than we can accomplish in a one-day seminar. This is also the one section of the workshop that is more lecture-driven. If you feel uncomfortable with this area, then you can choose to hit it very lightly for now, but do know that you will need to obtain the knowledge and pass it on to your group if you want to do your very best in performance.

The Stage

First, let's begin with the stage (see diagram). There are nine basic areas of the stage (some theatres use more but for most church productions nine will be sufficient). These areas serve as your compass to navigate the stage. Stage directions are always given from the perspective of the actor standing onstage, facing the audience. Stage right is to the actor's right; stage left is to the actor's left. Downstage is the area closest to the audience. Upstage is the area farthest away from the audience. Some areas are stronger than others. Obviously, the closer to the audience and the more centered you are on the stage will establish a stronger connection with the audience. So, from strongest to weakest, the areas are: Down Center, Center, Down Right, Down Left, Right, Left, Up Right, Up Left. (There is a larger picture of this diagram in the back of the book. You may want to duplicate it and use it as a handout to the participants.)

Key
C = center
D = down
U = up
R = right
L = left

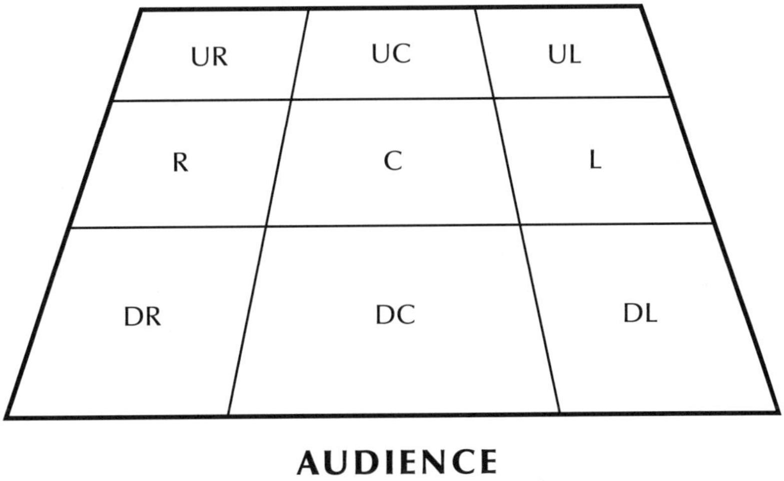

DO THIS: After explaining the stage areas, ask for a volunteer to come to the front of the room. Establish an area that will be your stage and then call out random stage areas and see if the volunteer can move to the correct location. Try it with several volunteers to make sure the actors understand.

Stance

Now that we understand the stage and stage directions, we need to talk about proper stance onstage. It is very important for actors to understand this simple rule: Always stand onstage with your upstage foot forward. That is to say your foot that is farthest away from the audience should be slightly ahead of the one that is closest to the audience (see diagram).

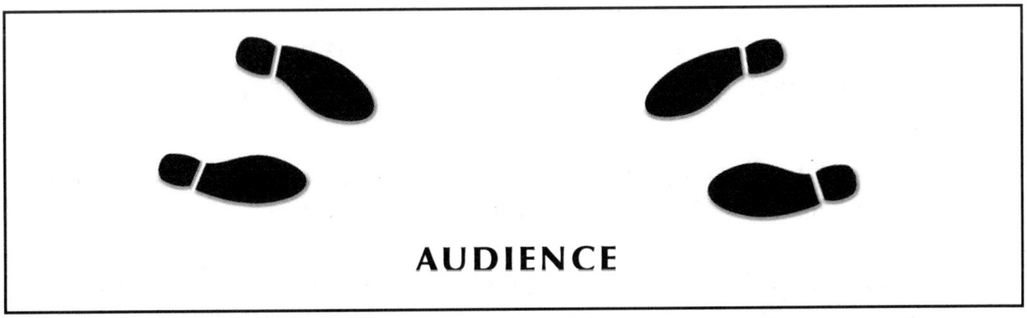

Notice that I did not say, "your right foot is ahead of your left foot" or "your left foot is ahead of your right." If I were facing left onstage then my left foot would be ahead, but if I were facing right, then my right foot would be ahead. Standing this way keeps you open to the audience, helping to avoid the tendency to turn your back to the audience.

Actors rarely directly face an audience. Usually they are talking and relating to other people onstage. The idea is for the audience to feel like they are peeking into a room or a scene through an invisible wall—often referred to as the "fourth wall."

Turning

A simple thing like turning onstage often becomes confusing. However, if you keep a few simple rules in mind you should be able to master it with a bit of practice:

- Your first step onto the stage is always made with your upstage foot.
- Always remember to stop with your upstage foot forward.
- Always turn toward the audience, not away from them.
- Avoid taking several little steps to make the turn. One move, pivoting on the balls of your feet, is all that it takes.
- After you have turned, again make your first step with your upstage foot.

DO THIS: Have the actors pair up and do a drill on stance and turning. If room permits, try having them partner with a person on the other side of the room and the whole group can do this at the same time. If space does not permit, then just do a few pairs at a time.

SAY THIS: I want you and your partner to first establish where the audience is, and then walk toward each other, remembering to step off on your upstage foot. Once you meet (center stage), stop with your upstage foot forward and shake hands. Then, remembering to turn toward the audience, pivot on the balls of your feet so you are facing the opposite direction and then step off on the upstage foot again as you go back to your side of the room.

Sitting

We all have "signatures" when it comes to our personal idiosyncrasies. You can often identify someone by the sound of their footsteps, the way they sigh or a certain posture—even from a great distance. The same is true of the way we sit; both the act of sitting and the posture we assume once seated. First, let's see what we all look like.

SAY THIS: Everyone stand up (wait for them to stand). Now, sit back down (wait for them to sit). Now do it again. Stand up (wait). Sit down.

Now, share observations about how people sit. Some fall into the chair, some reach back and feel for the chair, some look over their shoulders before sitting, and some people bend over from the waist before lowering themselves into the chair. (You can demonstrate these if you like.)

SAY THIS: Everyone stand up again. Stand nice and straight with good posture. Now, keeping your back as straight as possible, lower yourself onto the edge of the front of the chair and then slide back into the chair.

DO THIS: Have people again establish where the audience is and practice approaching their chair from several steps away. They should see the chair from

a distance; then when they arrive at the chair, let the backs of their legs "find" the chair by brushing against it. Then without looking at it, they lower themselves into the chair. Try this several times.

⌘ *Side Coach: Remember to step off on your upstage foot. Turn toward the audience. Trust the chair without looking at it.*

Now that they have gotten into the chair, take a moment to talk about how they position themselves once seated:

Men: While many men like to sit with their legs spread wide apart, this looks terrible from the audience. Men should have their legs closer together with about the width of their hand as space between their knees. Men may also cross their legs, but cross them so the middle of the calf rests on the knee rather than crossing them so the ankle rests on the knee. This will look much better.

Women: Obviously, keep legs together and preferably cross legs at the ankle. This is both a pleasing and modest position onstage.

Remember, we are talking neutral here. The character we are playing may dictate a different way to stand, walk, and sit.

Gestures

People generally fall into one extreme or the other when it comes to gesturing onstage: either they gesture too much or not at all. I don't usually advocate "planning" or "rehearsing" gestures. Most actors will discover the appropriate gestures as they discover the character. But still, there are a few rules to keep in mind.

- Make most of your gestures with your upstage hand. This helps keep you open to the audience and prevents you from blocking your face with your gestures.
- Avoid "double-pumping." This is both hands doing the same thing at the same time.
- Gestures need to have motivation—just like all movement onstage. There needs to be a reason for the gesture.
- When not gesturing, simply relax your arms and your hands at the sides of your body. Avoid the habit of always crossing your arms or putting your hands in your pockets. These habits tend to make you look uncomfortable onstage and subtly say to the audience: "I don't know what to do with my hands so I think I'll put them in my pockets."

Tip: If possible, always give actors a hand prop. It is amazing how many problems are solved by giving actors something to put in their hands. The prop can be something that helps identify who the character is or what they do. It will become an extension of their character. You will see your actors become much more comfortable onstage once they have a hand prop.

DEBRIEF

Try these questions for discussion:

Q: Did you learn anything about yourself as we went through this section?

Q: What will be the hardest part for you in turning these basics into habits?

Q: Will knowing these basics change the way you watch plays in the future?

CHAPTER 6

Acting Basics—Eye Focus

Our eyes, while a very small part of our body, are extremely important in the communication process, both in real life and onstage. The next section will help the group understand just how important they are. I like to set up the next exercise without telling the group what it is about. They will figure it out before the exercise is done.

3-Way Conversation

PURPOSE: To show how our eyes communicate. To help each of us evaluate comfort levels in personal communication.

SAY THIS: Everybody get a partner (encourage them to get someone they have not worked with yet). Spread out over the room—try to find some space so you are not to close to another team. Now, sit either in a chair or on the floor back to back with your partner. There are three phases to this exercise.

Phase one is to simply begin having a conversation with your partner. Talk about whatever you want. Just remember to remain back to back.

DO THIS: Let them converse for at least two minutes. You want to give them enough time to get the conversation going. Make observations about comfort zones and notice who is enjoying this phase and who is not.

SAY THIS: OK, stop! Now phase two. I want you to turn and face each other and continue your conversation; however, you are not allowed to make eye contact with your partner. Look wherever you like, except into their eyes. Go.

DO THIS: Once again, allow them to talk for a couple of minutes. Give them enough time to get used to the new setup. Continue to make observations as before.

SAY THIS: Stop. Now, for phase three, this time I want you to continue your conversation, but never take your eyes off of your partner's eyes. You are eyeball to eyeball the whole time.

DO THIS: Again, let them talk for a few minutes as you observe the different responses to the exercise.

After they have talked for a bit, stop them and have them turn their attention on you for a discussion. This exercise is very effective in helping people see just how important the eyes are in our communication.

▼ *Variation: One thing you will inevitably hear is that none of the three phases is like "real life." In order to give the group a chance at "real life," I sometimes have them do a fourth phase of, "just have a normal conversation." What is fun about doing that is*

DEBRIEF

You want people to begin to see that our eyes say things that go beyond words. So many truisms will come out in this discussion. You want the group to identify the fact that such things as honesty, love, hate, concern, confusion, intimacy, and more are all communicated through the eyes.

Q: Which of the three phases was most comfortable? Uncomfortable? Why? (Note: There is not a right or wrong answer here. You will find that usually there are people who prefer one of the phases over another and often for very different reasons.)

Q: What does eye contact suggest?

Q: When you see really intense eye contact in a play or a movie what is about to happen? (Note: could be a kiss; could be a fight!)

Q: What does this exercise have to do with acting?

the group will be so focused on trying to figure out what normal is, that the fourth phase really is not normal after all!

Eye Isolation

This exercise is optional, but a good one to further illustrate the power the eyes have in communicating ideas and emotions.

PURPOSE: To increase awareness of the eyes and their role in communication.

DO THIS: In advance, prepare a list of common emotions. You will want at least four. Here are some examples: fear, love, hate, and boredom.

SAY THIS: Find a partner (or stay with the same partner from the previous exercise). For simply a point of reference, assign one person as "A" and one as "B." (Give them a moment to do this.) Person "A" is going to be the "sender" and person "B" is the receiver. Now, I am going to give the "A's" an emotion. They are then going to cover their face below the eyes with a piece of paper and using only their eyes, and without speaking, try to convey that emotion to the "B's." The "B's" are to see if they can guess the emotion. All the "A's" come up here and I will give you your emotion.

DO THIS: All the "A's" come to you and you assign them the first word (fear). Send them back to their partner and give them a couple minutes to try to communicate the word. Then repeat the exercise, switching roles and giving a word to the "B's." Let each person do two words.

⌘ *Side Coach: Remember to use only your eyes. Concentrate; don't allow yourself to get distracted or get the giggles.*

▼ *Variation: As person "A" is sending the emotion, have person "B" communicate back with their eyes the same emotion. Now try it with person "B" sending back a contrasting emotion.*

DEBRIEF

Ask these questions:

Q: How many of you were successful in communicating the emotion to your partner?

Q: If you guessed the wrong emotion, how far off were you?

Q: Did you notice other parts of your body getting involved in the communication, almost involuntarily? What can you learn from this?

A few more notes on eye contact and focus onstage that should be discussed:

- Actors are often uncertain where to focus their eyes when they are onstage and not speaking. It is easy to figure out in the two-person conversation that you make eye contact with the person you are talking to. But if you are onstage and not part of the conversation . . . what then? As a general rule, eyes should follow the dialog. This is how you communicate to the audience that you are listening—by focusing on the person doing the talking. If you are not supposed to be involved in the conversation, then your character should have another reason for being on the stage, and the eyes are occupied in communicating that purpose (i.e., reading a magazine, eating, conversing silently with another character not in the audible dialog).

- Avoid "floor stabbing" and "ceiling stabbing." This is where you focus your eyes either up or down instead of at the person you are talking to. Sometimes an actor will do this momentarily, as if thinking to themselves, and as long as it is only a brief look away that is acceptable. Some actors turn this into a habit. It is almost as if they are looking for their lines on the floor or ceiling and this is to be avoided. This is especially noticeable in longer lines and monologues.
- As we have already discussed, your eyes and your facial expressions are powerful communicators. The audience needs to see your thoughts mirrored on your face. While we don't want you to look at the audience (remember the fourth wall), we do want them to see your face in order to know what you are thinking. So make sure your face is up and open to the audience.

CHAPTER 7

Acting Basics—Voice Projection

You will notice that up to this point, very little of our time and emphasis has had anything to do with speaking. This is intentional, to help drive home the point that acting is a visual medium and what we say with our bodies is as important as what we say with our mouths. Now we shift to some vocal emphasis. We can have great body control, but if we can't be heard, then it is all for naught (unless we are preparing to become a mime!). Stage acting has changed over the years. It used to be that actors never relied on microphones to be heard. Actors were trained to project and prided themselves in their ability to be heard without amplification. Today, almost every actor uses a microphone. While this technology has many benefits, it is still important for actors to know how to project their voices. Murphy's law does apply: "things will go wrong." Even the best sound equipment can't compensate for an actor that speaks too softly.

Breathing

PURPOSE: To show the importance of proper breathing and its relationship to a strong voice onstage.

SAY THIS: Everybody stand. Now, take a big deep breath and then exhale. OK, now do it again.

DO THIS: While they are taking their breaths, watch for signs of incorrect breathing; it should be easy to spot. Correct breathing comes from the diaphragm. When a person takes an incorrect deep breath, their shoulders go up and their chest pumps out. This does not give you good breath support. Conversely, if a person breathes from the diaphragm, their stomach expands and they are able to hold much more air. After you have spotted some examples of good and bad breathing, explain the difference to the group.

SAY THIS: I want you to place your hand just below your rib cage and at the top of your stomach. Now breathe in and breathe out and see if you can feel your stomach going in and out on each breath. Think in terms of filling your body with air, filling from the bottom up. It might help you to inhale as if you were sipping through a straw. Try inhaling slowly while I count to 5, then hold your breath for a 5-count, and then exhale slowly over a 5-count. Ready, inhale. 1 . . . 2 . . . 3 . . . 4 . . . 5; hold, 1 . . . 2 . . . 3 . . . 4 . . . 5; exhale, 1 . . . 2 . . . 3 . . . 4 . . . 5. You can practice this at home and gradually increase the numbers. This will help you increase your breathing capacity and combat shortness of breath onstage.

Here are some other things we can try together:

- Pant like a dog (do it); feel the stomach kick as you pant.
- Say with me: "HA, HA, HA." (Do several times.) Strive for a nice, loud accented punch on each "HA."

Notice that when we do this, we are not screaming. Screaming affects the throat and is most definitely the wrong way to project. Screaming will result in a sore throat and damaged voice. Proper projection may make your body tired, but will put very little strain on the voice.

Tip: Sometimes you will encounter an actor who is unaware of the volume of their own voice, and no matter how many times you tell them to project, they will speak at the same volume. You might try taking your group outside and pair them up in the parking lot. Have them recite words to a nursery rhyme back and forth to each other, but with each line they speak, they take one more step backward away from each other. Sometimes this helps them to be aware of the need to pump up the volume.

CHAPTER 8

Acting Basics—Diction

You can have great projection, but if we can't understand you because you have bad diction or you are talking too fast, then we have a problem. These next couple of exercises will help make us more aware of the need for good diction.

Pencil in the Mouth

PURPOSE: To force clear articulation of words and to force slower speech.

DO THIS: Make sure each person has a pen or pencil.

SAY THIS: Take your pencil and place it lengthwise (like you're eating an ear of corn) between your front teeth. Gently bite down to hold it in place. Now turn to the person next to you and begin having a conversation. Make sure you can be clearly understood as you talk around the obstacle in your mouth. (Let them try this for a couple minutes.) Take the pencil out of your mouth and continue the conversation as if the pencil was still in your mouth—not with clenched teeth, but making your tongue and lips work just as hard as they were when you had the pencil in your mouth.

DEBRIEF

Ask the group the following questions:

Q: What effect did the pencil have on your speech?

Q: Could you tell a difference in the way you talked once you removed the pencil?

Tongue Twisters

PURPOSE: To force good articulation and rate of speech.

DO THIS: Prepare in advance several well-known tongue twisters. (You could write these on a chalkboard or have them on a handout.) Here are a few you can use:

- Rubber baby buggy bumpers.
- She sells seashells by the seashore.

The shells she sells are surely seashells.
So if she sells shells on the seashore
I'm sure she sells seashore shells.

- How much wood would a woodchuck chuck
if a woodchuck could chuck wood?
He would chuck, he would, as much as he could,
and chuck as much wood as a woodchuck would
if a woodchuck could chuck wood.
- A skunk sat on a stump and thunk the stump stunk,
but the stump thunk the skunk stunk.
- Peter Piper picked a peck of pickled peppers.
Did Peter Piper pick a peck of pickled peppers?
If Peter Piper picked a peck of pickled peppers,
where's the peck of pickled peppers Peter Piper picked?
- Six thick thistle sticks. Six thick thistles stick.

Have the group say these out loud in unison. Try varying the rate; getting faster without messing up. These are good for a few laughs but also serve to make the point.

DEBRIEF

Have a discussion about the importance of good diction. Identify common words that are often mispronounced or slurred in real life but from onstage would be hard to understand. One I often use is, "Let's go eat." In real life conversation it is often said fast and run together in one word like this: "lesogoeet." Onstage in a large auditorium that might sound like, "squeet."

Hopefully this example and others like it will help your actors see the need for good, clear enunciation!

CHAPTER 9

Acting Basics—Memorization

I have to admit that memorizing lines is probably my least favorite thing to do as an actor. I dare say that most actors I know would agree! (However, I do know a few strange people who actually like to memorize!) Memorization can be hard work—no question. But with a few easy-to-learn techniques and with the right frame of mind, it can be some of your most productive time in preparing for a role. It is important to understand the difference between merely memorizing your lines and "owning your lines." An actor's goal is to know the lines so well that you don't have to stop and think, "What comes next?" The focus should be on character, not lines, when it comes time for performance. This idea of owning lines is brought home in the following discussion.

SAY THIS: What are some things you know by heart? Things you can recite without stopping to ask, "What is the next word or sentence?"

DO THIS: Likely answers to the above question will be: The Lord's Prayer, The Pledge of Allegiance, "Mary Had a Little Lamb," the alphabet, etc. Point out that these are things they own. Wouldn't it be nice if we knew our lines in a play as well as we know these things?

Steps in Memorizing

Here are some tried and true steps in memorizing a script.

- Read the script, read the script, read the script! At the risk of being redundant—read the script. Read it first to get a good understanding of the story. Read it again to gain insight into your character. Read it again for understanding of other characters and their interaction with your character. Read it until you can tell the story of the script in your own words.
- Highlighting your lines so they stand out on the page.
- Using a blank sheet of paper, cover all the lines and slide the paper down—a line at a time—as you work on each of your lines.
- Memorize out loud. Say your lines and the cue lines (the other person's lines) out loud.
- Only after you can respond with the correct line, word for word, do you move on to the next line.
- Memorize on your feet. Keeping your body moving gets your blood pumping, helping to keep you alert and focused.

The methods above are not the only methods that work. Many people have great success using a tape recorder. This is a great method, especially when finding someone to run lines with you is inconvenient. If using a tape recorder, be sure to record not only your lines, but the cue lines as well, so you will be accustomed to hearing and learning those cues!

You need to be aware that memorization comes in phases. There is the "on paper phase," where you are working from reading the lines. You need to graduate from this to the "audible phase," where you run the lines with another person to get you accustomed to hearing the lines. Next there is the "with movement phase," where you incorporate your blocking (stage blocking is the term used for the movement given to an actor) and stage action with the lines. The final phase is "What will you really do in front of a live audience?" This is where we find out if you will succumb to stage fright or be able to truly enjoy being in the moment and acting in front of people. I find it a good idea to have a small audience of family and friends at a dress rehearsal in order to test the performers in this area, as well as allowing them to experience a live audience before the real thing on opening night. Another option would be to perform the show before a small group, like a Sunday School class or at a retirement home.

Tip: Line memorization is a great place to practice the basic movements we talked about earlier. Practice stepping off on the upstage foot and then turning toward the audience. This will help make those simple movements a habit! If the actor knows the stage blocking ahead of time, then practicing the blocking in conjunction with the line memorization helps to learn it all at once!

One question that inevitably comes up on the subject of memorization is, "Do I have to memorize my lines word for word?" The answer to this is always YES! Why? Here are a few good reasons:

- You are not the playwright (well . . . unless you are the playwright). In most situations you are performing a published work and so copyright law will usually prohibit you from making changes without the author/publisher's consent.
- Learning lines also involves learning cue lines. If the actor I am onstage with changes their line, then there is a good chance he/she will throw me off track with the paraphrased line. You should never surprise other actors onstage by doing or saying things that were not rehearsed, and paraphrasing a line is a sure way to surprise your fellow actors.
- One reason actors will want to change a line is usually this excuse: "I would never say it that way." My response is, "So what? You are not the character. The character would say it that way, so you need to let the character say it that way—not you!"
- On the rare occasion where a line change is permitted (localizing a play, adapting for gender, etc.), any line changes are agreed upon in advance so they become a permanent part of the script.

One of the biggest fears an actor has is forgetting his/her lines. So let's address that. What should you do if you forget your lines or if you are onstage with someone who has forgotten their lines?

- Don't panic. I know that is easier said than done! If you follow the memorization methods outlined above, you will know the story and thus, know what is supposed to happen next. Stop and take a breath, and recall what you just said and what is supposed to happen next. Often this will get you right back on track. One reason that actors go blank is because they stop being "in the moment." They get distracted by thinking ahead or replaying a scene that did not go well and suddenly they are not really listening and connected to what is happening now.
- In the memorization methods described above, you were to say not only your line out loud, but the cue line as well. One of the benefits of this is that you will discover that you have actually memorized the cue line—even though you were not consciously trying to do so. This is of great benefit onstage. If you are onstage with someone who has gone blank you have several options:
    - Take their line for them, paraphrasing it slightly to make it your own.
    - Ask them a question that helps them recall what they are supposed to say.
    - Drop hints of information in ad-libbed lines that help remind the actor of what they are supposed to say.

Remember, the goal when things go wrong is to get back on track—not invent a whole new script. A common tendency when an actor blanks is to just say any line they can think of, even if that means jumping ahead several pages. This only escalates the problem—now not only do you have to try to get back on track, but you also have to figure out how to go back and pick up the information in the script that has been skipped. Better to take a few seconds of painful silence than to leave out important information that confuses or thwarts the storyline. Often the few seconds of silence will seem like an eternity to you but the audience may not even notice.

DEBRIEF

This is often a section that generates quite a bit of discussion. The fear of blanking onstage is very real. Take time here to allow people to voice their concerns and encourage each other in this area.

Finally, remember that old TV commercial for deodorant that used the slogan "Never let them see you sweat?" The audience should never know that you made a mistake. Learn to cover your mistakes. Make your mistakes look like they were "supposed to happen that way." Say the wrong line with gusto and then worry about fixing it. Don't say, "Oops!" If you walk on the stage at the wrong time, cover your mistake by making it look like you were supposed to enter then. The audience will usually never be aware of your mistakes—and thus, you should never talk about them with anyone except the cast. You want the audience to believe what they are seeing is really happening—when you talk about the things that go wrong with the audience members, you are ruining the very effect you were trying to create.

CHAPTER 10

Acting Basics—Characterization

Now the fun begins. Up to this point most of the basics we have talked about are just that—the basics. The real fun and creative part of being an actor is in creating believable characters onstage. This is where we get to use our imaginations; where we revert back to what many of us did so well in our childhood—pretend. As we get older, we tend to lose the knack for playing and pretending. We view that as childishness. But, the very freedom that children have to lose themselves in a make-believe world is the very essence of real and believable characters onstage. We need to recapture that!

"Being" not "Acting"

PURPOSE: To free our imaginations and move beyond stereotypes to create believable characters.

DO THIS: In setting up this exercise, it is important that you not give any preparation time to the group for the first phase. Part of the learning experience in this exercise is the contrast between the lack of prep time for the first phase contrasted with prep time for the second phase.

SAY THIS: Without thinking too much about it, I want everybody to pretend that you are 80 years old. Now get up and mill about the room and talk to each other as 80-year-old people.

DO THIS: Give the group about 3-5 minutes to play with this. During this time, observe what they are doing. If your group is typical, you will see a lot of people doing pretty much the same thing: stooped over posture, trembling hands, slight limp, and shaky voice. When you ask them to stop, don't allow them to discuss the experience yet.

SAY THIS: Stop. OK, now everybody take a seat. Please spread out in the room so you are not too close to another person. I don't want you to be distracted by anyone during the next phase of this exercise. We are going to become the 80-year-old person again, but this time we are going to approach it differently. I am going to give you a series of questions and statements designed to help you think through what it would be like to be 80 years old, and I want you to work through the answers in your imagination—don't answer out loud. This portion of the exercise is nonverbal on your part; I will be the only one talking. If some of the questions cause you to want to answer out loud or contribute a witty comment—resist the temptation. Please take the process seriously.

Before we begin you need to make a decision: are you going to be "you" at 80 years old or are you going to become another person? Now, before we begin, let me set the scene. I want you to imagine you are in your bedroom alone, sitting in front of a full-length mirror. Take a moment to see the room . . . because I will be asking you several questions about your body and physical condition. You might want to imagine you are sitting in your underwear—it's OK; there is no one else in the room. Also keep in mind that not everyone who is 80 years old is an invalid—some are very active, vital people. You decide what kind of person you want to create.

Allow your body to change as we consider each part of it. OK, close your eyes, take a deep breath and let's begin. (Note: After each question below, allow a moment of silence for them to think through the answer. It helps to make your voice as relaxing and soothing as possible so that people can focus their attention. These questions are only suggestions—feel free to create your own.)

- Start with your feet. What do they look like? See the color and texture of your skin. Scrunch your toes. Make your feet 80 years old.
- Move up to your ankles. Feel free to move them around. Do they move easily?
- Now move up to your calves and shins. Make them 80 years old.
- Next are your knees. As you age body parts that are joints, bear in mind that these are often problem spots in older people. Arthritis may be an issue. Is it for you?
- Move to your thighs. Make them 80 years old.
- Now your hips. Many older people end up having hip replacement surgery. How about you?
- Take a trip up your back. One vertebra at a time. Make it 80 years old. If you decide that you are stooped over, consider that the tension in being stooped over is up not down. You are trying to stand up straight; it's just that your body doesn't go and won't go any straighter.
- Consider your stomach and chest. Are there scars? Have you been under the surgeon's knife? Consider your internal organs. Your heart? Your stomach and digestive track? Your lungs? How is your breathing? Can you hear it?
- Look at your hands. See color and texture. How is your grip when you make a fist?
- Now consider your forearms, elbows, and upper arms. How does your skin hang on your upper arms?
- Now move to your shoulders. Square or rounded?
- See your neck. See how the skin hangs. See the wrinkles.
- How many chins can you count when you look in the mirror?
- Look at your face. Consider: Glasses? Hearing aids? False teeth? Wrinkles? Hair color? Baldness?

We could go on and on just on the physical aspects, but now let's move on to other areas for consideration.

- Are you married?
- If married, is your spouse living?
- Do you have children? How many?
- Where do you live? In your own home? Retirement home? With one of your children?
- Is immediate family nearby or far away? How often do you see family?
- What time do you get up in the morning?
- What do you eat for breakfast?
- What will you do today? Visit people? Volunteer? Stay home and watch TV?
- How would you describe yourself? Happy? A curmudgeon? Content? Bitter?
- What was the happiest day or time of your life?
- What was the saddest day or time of your life?
- How often do you see a doctor? Are you on a daily medication?
- Do you attend church?
- What is your relationship with God like?
- At the age of 80, you must have thought a lot about the end of your life. What are your general thoughts about death? Fear it? Looking forward to it?
- What are your regrets?
- Finish this sentence: "If I could do one more thing before I die it would be ______."

There are many more questions I could ask you, but you have enough now to move onto the next phase of this exercise. I want you to all imagine now that we are a room full of the 80-year-olds you have just been creating in your imaginations. We are going to imagine that we are all gathered together for a birthday party for a friend named Harold. You are all getting ready for his arrival at the party. When he comes in we will sing "Happy Birthday" to him. OK, let's get ready. Go!

DO THIS: Let them get up and move about the room. You might want to give them some ideas to motivate them. Allow enough time for them to really get into the character and interact with each other. After a few minutes, tab somebody to be "Harold" and have him enter the room so everyone can sing "Happy Birthday."

⌘ ***Side Coach:*** *Greet your friends, some who you have not seen for a long time. Introduce people to each other. Discuss how you know Harold. Somebody needs to organize the group for Harold's arrival. Harold is here!*

▼ ***Variation:*** *The above exercise can also be tweaked and adapted to different ages. Try having the group become all 5-year-olds. Another adaptation of the exercise is to have the group become a group from an era in history, i.e., have them all be the Israelites being led into the wilderness by Moses.*

DEBRIEF

Discuss with the group the difference between the first time they were 80 and the second time. What made the difference? How many were becoming "themselves" at 80? What is the difference between a caricature and a real person? Share observations and contrast between the first and second phase.

Character Analysis Worksheet

Included in the handouts at the end of the book is a "Character Analysis Worksheet." Photocopy and hand these out to the group for discussion. These sheets are intended to "jumpstart" the character analysis process. Developing believable characters onstage is a process that actors study and work on all the time and certainly takes more work and practice than can be accomplished in a short portion of a day-long workshop. However, if we can get the participants to ask two basic questions, we have done our job; "Who am I?" and "What do I want?" The next exercise will help to emphasize this point.

A/B Role-Play

PURPOSE: To introduce the idea of conflict in drama. To help actors discover "motivation" in preparing a scene.

SAY THIS: Everyone get a partner. Appoint one of you as person "A" and the other as person "B." As you know, drama is based on conflict. A play in which everyone agrees with each other all the time would be pretty boring. However, conflict doesn't necessarily mean fighting or arguing. It simply means that you want something and there is something keeping you from getting what you want—also referred to as an "obstacle." So, now we are going to give you a chance to work through some conflicts. First you need to know who you are—and the answer to this is, you are YOU! You are playing yourself, except as modified by the conflict (if I say you don't like coffee and you really do, then you have to pretend that you really don't like it!). Here is your first conflict:

- Person "A" has just won an all expenses paid trip to Europe. The vacation of a lifetime! You will be flown into Paris and then tour all over Europe for two weeks. You also get to bring one other person along and you have chosen your partner, Person "B."
- Person "B" is Person "A's" very good friend and would love nothing better than to go on this trip to Europe. However there is one slight problem—you

are terrified of flying. You have vowed to never get on an airplane for as long as you live. The very thought of getting on a plane makes you ill.

Now go ahead and role play.

DO THIS: While they act this out, you should observe and see how much they "get into" this exercise. You will notice that most will not be thinking about "acting" and thus are often very natural and uninhibited. They will be using body language, facial expressions, gestures, vocal inflections, and, in general, do a very believable job of acting. This is all good stuff and needs to be affirmed. So stop them and affirm them. Also, point out how easy it was to do this once they knew what their purpose was and totally understood the conflict. Make sure they get the connection between that and working on a play.

Then go on and do another one. Here is a suggestion:

SAY THIS: Let's do another one:

- Person "B" is single and just about 6 weeks ago met Mr. (or Miss) Right. This person is the person of your dreams. You are head-over-heels in love with each other. Even though you have only been dating for a few weeks, you have received (or given) a marriage proposal. You are on a fast track to get married. You can't wait to tell your friend, Person "A," all about it!
- Person "A" thinks this is a huge mistake. This is all happening way too fast. You think Person "B" needs to slow down—way down! Perhaps you know something about Mr. or Miss Right that if your friend knew, might just change their mind. Try to convince them not to go through with this crazy marriage plan!

After they have played this out, once again discuss this and share observations.

Open Scene

PURPOSE: To help actors discover motivation and meaning beyond what is explicit in written dialog.

DO THIS: There are short dialog samples in the handout section in this book. Photocopy them, making enough for each participant working in pairs. It is perfectly OK that several pairs will have the same dialog—in fact, that makes this exercise even more interesting. Have the actors partner up and then distribute the dialogs.

SAY THIS: As you are learning today, there is more to acting than just simply memorizing and speaking lines. Acting involves our bodies, our eyes, our imaginations, and more. The dialogs you have in your hands are out of context. Just reading them raises all kinds of who, what, where, when, and why questions. I want you and your partner to answer those questions. This is called the subtext. Discover or make up who and where these people are. Why are they saying the things they say? Give the scene a context. Then I want you to memorize the lines (the scenes are very short) and then you will perform them for the group. Your performance in context should "fill in the blanks" for the audience. However, you are only allowed to say what is on the page. You may not add any lines or words. You can and should add action. Keep in mind that you may need long pauses between lines and possibly even in the middle of a line in order for your context to be communicated. You have about 10 minutes to work on this and then the performance will begin.

DO THIS: Let them go to work. You may want to walk around and eavesdrop on the teams as they work, to make sure they are understanding the assignment. After the 10 minutes are up, call everyone together and have groups take turns performing the scenes. Affirm all the different interpretations that come out of the scenes. This exercise usually opens a lot of people's eyes in terms of understanding the difference between just saying words and acting from an understanding of context and motivation.

▼ *Variation: It can be great fun to assign actual biblical characters to the dialogs and see what they do with them. Don't tell the audience who they are, but see if they can guess based on what the actors do with the scenes. Examples: Adam and Eve, David and Goliath, Samson and Delilah, Mary and Joseph, Jesus and Judas.*

DEBRIEF

Discuss how they decided on the context. How did the context affect or change the way a line was said (especially if there were very different interpretations of the same scene)?

Story Improvisations

If time permits, give the actors one more opportunity to try to put it all together—body control, movement, eye contact, projection, diction, and characterization. A great way to do this is with story improvisations.

PURPOSE: To allow the actors to be creative and make up scenes. To practice the acting skills they have learned in the workshop.

DO THIS: Prepare in advance a list of locations that can be used as the basis for a simple story. You will need one location for each group of four or five people. Here is a list you can use (or make up your own): parking lot, grocery store, hotel lobby, police station, amusement park, classroom.

Break the participants up into groups of 4 or 5 people (or use the same animal groups formed at the beginning of the workshop).

SAY THIS: Now you are going to do a little group improvisation. I want you to make up and act out a simple story. I do mean simple; don't make this complicated. A story has a beginning, a middle, and an end. Establish a who and a what. I will give you the "where" and you do the rest. These stories should only last about 3 minutes. Keep it simple. Each person in your group should have a distinct character and at least one line of dialog. You don't need to write it out. It is improvisation; just make it up as you go, like you did in the A/B Role Play exercise. You will have about 5-10 minutes to prepare and then we will come together for performance.

DO THIS: Go around to each group and assign the location. While they are figuring out their stories you should listen and observe to make sure every group is understanding the exercise. You might need to give some simple story examples; i.e., a man is shopping, he sees another person shoplifting. He confronts the man who denies he did anything wrong. The clerk is called, who then calls the cops and they take the man away in handcuffs. After the preparation, call the group together for performance. Give plenty of affirmation and perhaps some mild critique after each performance. The critique should point out reminders about things like projection, basic staging (could we see everyone?), and motivation.

CHAPTER 11

Putting It All Together

If you made it this far, take a deep breath, pat yourself on the back and say a prayer of thanksgiving. You did it! The hard part of the workshop is over.

You might want to go back and revisit Chapter 2 and the section titled, "What Does It Take to Make It Work?" Before you send everyone home, it is a good idea to outline what happens next! Here would be a great time to craft a mission statement. Identify the purpose of your drama ministry. Are you primarily focused on drama in the worship service? Will you be mainly using drama for special occasions (Christmas and Easter)? Is touring and/or outreach your main goal? Knowing this is essential to planning your ministry.

How are you going to be organized? Will the person who directs the plays also be the organizer of all the drama events or will that responsibility be shared? How often will you meet? Will your meetings be training, rehearsal or both? Will you do social things as a group? (Going to see plays as a group is a great learning and bonding experience!) Will you include prayer and devotional time in your meetings (highly recommended)?

One thing to keep in mind is that drama ministries only seem to flourish when they have the payoff of performance. Set up a schedule of performances as soon as you can. The team will be excited to know that there is a performance looming. They won't want to come to regular meetings if there are no performances upcoming.

Hopefully, this has been a great launching pad for your ministry. May God bless your talents and your service to Him . . . dramatically!

For Additional Reading

Drama Ministry
Steve Pederson
Zondervan Publishing

What to Do with the Second Shepherd on the Left
Deborah Craig-Claar
Lillenas Drama Resources

Incorporating Drama in Worship
Mike Gray
Lillenas Drama Resources

Improvisation Starters
Phillip Bernardi
Better Way Books

Stage Diagram

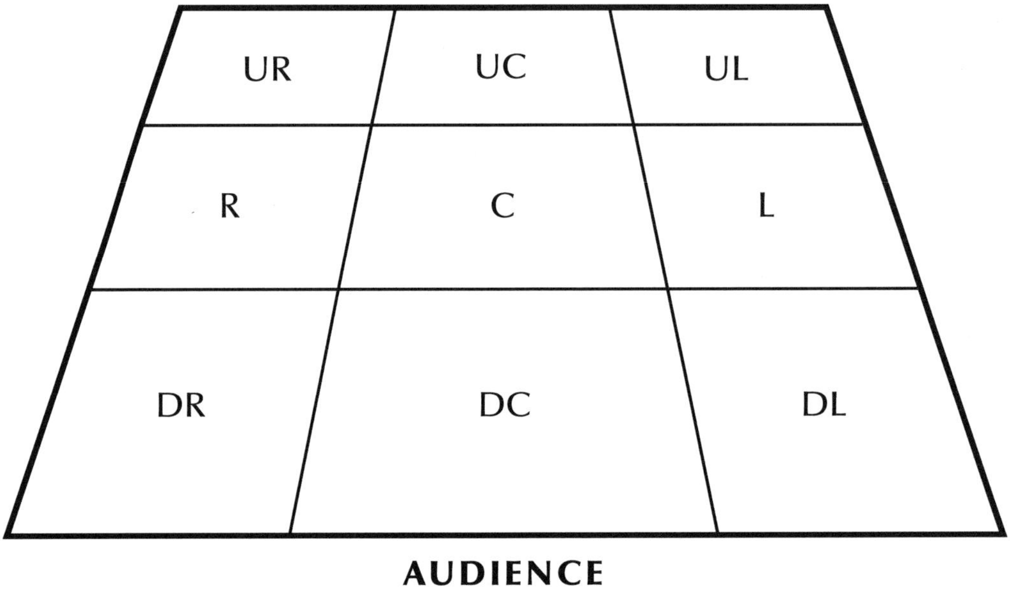

Key
C = center
D = down
U = up
R = right
L = left

Character Analysis Worksheet

Analyze the script to determine these clues to your character.

What the character does.

What the character says.

What the other characters say about him/her and their purpose in saying it.

What actions are suggested in the character's lines.

What comments and descriptions are offered in the playwright's stage directions.

Based on the information in the script and *clues derived from the director's interpretation of the play,* it is now the actor's task to make the character a real person.

History

Consider the background and history of the character:

- Name
- Age
- Birthplace
- Appearance
- Parents
- Siblings
- Religion
- Education
- World history
- Ethnic background
- Occupation
- Athletics
- Physical problems
- Hobbies
- Skills
- Spouse
- Children
- Social standing
- Deaths
- Honors

Emotional Makeup

Consider the emotional makeup of the character. Evaluate the character in the following areas (feel free to add to the list). Consider the how's and why's of each area that apply.

- Aggressive
- Passive
- Angry
- Impulsive
- Happy-go-lucky
- Logical
- Depressed
- Vindictive
- Reflective
- Tactful
- Direct
- Fearful
- Hopeful
- Apathetic
- Lonely
- Anxious
- Impatient
- Wishy washy
- Evasive
- Loving

Questions to Consider

What does my character want?
What is my character willing to do to get it?
How does my character feel about the other characters in the play?
Is my character a protagonist or an antagonist?
Does my character like himself/herself? Why or why not?
Does my character change during the play? How and why?
What motivates or drives my character?
How does my character spend a typical day?
Is my character on attack or defense?
What are my character's greatest strengths? Weaknesses?
Why and how is my character important to this play?
Which of the other characters in the play is your character's favorite? Least favorite? Why?
What are my character's goals and aspirations?
How is my character different from myself? In what ways is he/she the same?

Sample Dialogs

Sample Dialog #1*

A: What are you doing here?

B: I brought this.

A: Yes, I see.

B: Good.

A: Now what?

B: Maybe it's time to go.

A: Oh.

*Dialog #1 written by Tom Long, *Friends of the Groom.* Used by permission.

Sample Dialog #2

A: So now what do we do?

B: I'm really hungry.

A: Well, what about me?

B: It won't be much longer.

A: Great!

B: Come on!

A: I'll start a fire.

Sample Dialog #3

A: I thought I'd find you here.

B: I can't stand it!

A: What are you going to do?

B: I know what I'd like to do!

A: That won't solve anything.

B: I'd feel better.

A: No, you wouldn't. Is this the right time?

B: Not yet.

Sample Dialog #4

A: You always said I could ask you anything.

B: Yeah, but not that . . . that's different.

A: How? You did it, didn't you?

B: Why do you jump to that conclusion?

A: Because of that.

B: Oh, I forgot about that. Maybe I should hide it.

A: Here. It's OK. It's safe with me.

The Play Is the Thing
by Chuck Neighbors

First published in "Worship Leader Magazine," November 1995

"I hate sketches!"

The words startled me as I craned my neck in the darkened auditorium to see who had uttered them. I was startled a second time to see that the complaint came from the mouth of a respected Christian artist whose name many of you would instantly recognize.

He was not the only one to echo those sentiments at a drama conference I recently attended. Indeed, not only at this conference but throughout the growing ranks of the current "Christian drama" movement, there seems to be a love/hate relationship developing over the most popular utilization of drama in the church —the sketch (aka: short play, vignette, and the most hated by the theatre purest— "skit").

I was reluctant to agree with the sentiments of the person who spoke those words of contempt—after all, I have written several "sketches" myself—but at the moment, I felt pretty much the same way. I'm sure some of the feelings were due to the fact that it was a three-day conference filled with performances dominated by sketches. To those who are devotees of the stage, sketches are like candy on the menu of all that the theatre has to offer. I like candy in small amounts but not as the main meal—eat a meal's worth of M&M's and say hello to Maalox. To put it another way, sketches are the equivalent of the TV sit-com in the theatre world. Although I enjoy watching *Everybody Loves Raymond*, I don't think I could sit through three straight hours of reruns. I use the word "reruns" intentionally, as there is a certain sameness to much that is done through sketches. When it comes to sketches—like sit-coms—it seems there really is "nothing new under the sun." You are left with the feeling of, "Gee, haven't we seen that one before?"

"But wait," you say, "I thought all you drama types were excited about the way the church has finally opened up to drama." Yes, we are! The church is finally opening up to this dynamic art form and "drama types" are thrilled at the possibilities. But let's explore those possibilities—otherwise we run the risk of letting the sketch become the sole definition of Christian drama in our age.

Now, having said all of that, let's deal with reality. And the reality is that, for now, to paraphrase Shakespeare: "The sketch is the thing." While many of us may long for the day that the church catches a bigger vision for the dramatic arts, we need to do our very best with what we are given. And that is the sketch. It is being used primarily in two ways by the local church. The most common is the style made popular by churches such as Willow Creek Community Church in the Chicago area. These sketches usually precede the sermon and are topical, designed to raise an issue that will be addressed in the sermon. The sketches are open-ended and often humorous.

The second is more overtly worship oriented. These sketches are popular in more traditional/liturgical settings. Here the sketch may serve as a Call to Worship, Prayer Meditation or Benediction. These performances are often more serious and may not even be a sketch at all—incorporating other forms of artistic expression such as readers' theatre, poetry, and interpretive movement.

In order to produce drama, and in particular sketches, to the very best of our ability, let's consider some quality control criteria.

Identifying the Target

I recently attended two drama conferences where a good portion of the works presented were what I classify as plays designed to "preach to the choir." These plays bolstered consensus but did little to challenge the viewers. Granted, some of them were written and performed at a high level of competence. The audience responded positively with laughter and applause. But I question whether the sketches were appropriate for their audience.

In order to select the "right sketch," we have to know our audience. Is the audience a traditional vs. contemporary congregation? Is the service "seeker" targeted? What is the average age, socio-economic status and cultural background of the group?

After we have evaluated our audience, we should define our purpose in presenting the drama. What is the theme of the service? What do we want to communicate? What is our goal? What effect do we want to leave on the audience?

Perhaps this is good place to underscore the importance of a "team concept" in regard to your drama ministry. It is essential to have the support and input of the church staff—especially the pastor. Usually a drama team without the support of the church leadership is dead in the water. Only with a unified vision and purpose will your drama program flourish and grow. In most churches utilizing drama, there is an emphasis on designing the service around a specific theme. The music, drama, scripture, and sermon all have a common thread running through them. How can a drama team possibly complement this focus without the input of the pastor and other worship leaders?

Selecting the Play

Quite simply, a play is a story. What we are looking for in a play are, in essence, the same elements that make up a good story. At its most basic, we are looking for:

- An interesting story which contains a beginning, middle, and an end.
- Conflict. A story with no conflict is spelled B-O-R-I-N-G.
- Believable dialog—the characters should talk the way real people talk.
- An open ending. Perhaps the one major difference between most stories and

a good sketch is that often a sketch will end with an intentional lack of resolution (although, there are exceptions).

As previously mentioned, there are too many plays being done that "preach to the choir." I would like to suggest something that many may have a hard time reconciling in their concept of ministry: it should not be the goal of drama to preach. Yes, drama should communicate, challenge, foster identification, entertain, and stir us up. It may even carry the impact of a sermon, but it should never have preaching as its goal! Leave it to the pastor to preach. To use drama to preach is in essence to risk defeating the greatest strength of drama; to communicate without preaching!

I have read numerous sketches that should have ended well before they actually did. The playwright has a great scenario going—an interesting conflict with some good characters and sparkling dialog. But on page three, Joe Christian enters and says "just the right words" that suddenly solve the conflict and the characters all live "happily every after." Instead of ending the play with something we can think about and struggle with, Joe Christian gives us the "right answer." By doing so, he lets the audience off the hook. Those who agree with Joe say "amen." Those who aren't so sure find Joe's solution a little too pat.

Remember, we are talking primarily about sketches here—although some of these principles apply to longer plays as well. In my opinion, the sketches that lack a resolution are the best. Present a conflict that contains a "slice of life" and raises an issue, but don't tell me how to solve it. You can even point me in the right direction, but an open ending leaves me with a challenge.

Perhaps the best example of the power of a good sketch is in the parables of Jesus. He told His followers a short story, often ending it with a question. His listeners were left with something to think about and the parable raised even more questions in their minds. Often they would confront Jesus, asking Him to explain the parable. Sounds like a good model for the use of the sketch as a prelude to the sermon, doesn't it?

More often than not, sketches tend to be humorous. Generally this is good, as humor will cause an audience to drop their defenses. Once they laugh you know that they are identifying with the situation. One word of caution: keep the humor on a high level. Resist humor that goes for the gag. Often these funny bits are out of place with the story. Make the humor come from the story and/or the character. Don't go for the laugh just for the sake of the laugh. If you do, the audience remembers only the funny bit instead of the salient point of the play.

While humor is great, don't be afraid of doing the occasional totally serious drama. These can be very effective in churches that have become accustomed to having drama on a regular basis. Explore new styles and try to avoid ruts. Try mime, or readers' theatre for variety. Keep the audience wondering what you will do next week. Otherwise, they may start to think of you as the "sit-com" before the sermon.

One other consideration in selecting material is, of course, the issue of your group's talent and ability. Fortunately, you will find that most sketches are for smaller casts. It is very difficult to do drama on a regular basis with a very small talent pool. Be realistic in selecting material that your group can handle.

Resources

It is not surprising that many of the churches performing drama on a regular basis are writing their own material. It's impossible to find published plays that are going to hit your specific theme each and every week of the year. So, if you have the talent in your group to create your own scripts, it is probably the best option for on-target communication.

But what if you don't have your own budding Shakespeare in the fold? Thankfully, there is much more drama on the "market" than ever before, but not all of the new material meets the quality test. Just because a play is published doesn't necessarily mean that it is of superior quality. And even though a published play may deal with the topic that you need, it still may not be right for your specific situation. I'm afraid you cannot do a very effective job of play selection based on a short synopsis provided by the publisher. In other words, you will still need to do your homework, which means a lot of reading.

There are several publishers that are offering drama series specifically designed for worship. Among them are Baker Books, Lillenas, Word, and Zondervan (Willow Creek Resources). Check them out. Hopefully they can help you "get your act together."

In the meantime, let's keep exploring, improving and expanding this most effective medium of the arts. To finish the quote from Shakespeare: "The play is the thing wherein I'll catch the conscience of the king." Perhaps we'll capture a conscience or two for the King as well!

Redeeming Entertainment

Keynote Address, Drama Improvement Conference, October 2003
Sunset Presbyterian Church, Beaverton, Oregon

(Note from Chuck: This is what I consider the "meat" of the address. There were opening comments and a humorous story preceding what you are reading here.)

I want to say things tonight that will inspire, encourage, and challenge you. I realize that to speak to a group like this is, in essence, to "preach to the choir." But maybe that is not all bad. This is one choir that doesn't get together all that often, so maybe a little preaching to the choir is just what we need. To speak the truths of the things that we all agree on—to have those ideals reinforced and encouraged—is certainly not out of line for this gathering. Yet, I am not satisfied to have you walk out of here with a sort of "ho hum, same old same old" theme.

So I had to turn the question in on myself and ask, "What would I like to hear? What do I need to hear fleshed out a bit more?"

For too long I have felt the need to apologize to the church for the fact that what I do, what we do, as theatre artists, is to in fact entertain. I have had more conversations than I can count with people who want to challenge and even condemn the notion that doing drama on a Sunday morning in church is entertainment and that church should not be a place of entertainment. So tonight I am going to challenge that notion, rather than apologize for it as I have so often done in the past. Tonight, I want to redeem entertainment! First, to redeem the world—that is the feel-good part of my talk. Second, to talk about entertainment that is redeeming—that will be perhaps the challenge part of what I want to say tonight. And third, how in following our calling as entertainers for the cause of Christ, we can experience a measure of redemption not only for our art, but also for our souls.

Redeeming the Word "Entertainment"

Much of what I want to say tonight has to do with definitions. As actors and writers, we know that words mean things. According to the dictionary "entertainment," as pertaining to performance, has three distinct parts: to hold attention, to amuse, to divert.

To hold attention? Think about that part as I substitute and turn a phrase or two.

- The church should not be a place of entertainment—The church should not be a place that holds our attention. (Clearly some have succeeded if that is the goal.)
- This is a place of worship not a place of entertainment—This is a place of worship and not a place that holds our attention.

- I came to hear a sermon, not to have someone entertain me—I came to hear a sermon, not have someone hold my attention.

If entertainment means "holding attention," then it certainly is something to be desired by the church today.

I must admit that I thought my premise for this talk was in trouble when I got to the next word: to amuse. When you hear the world "amuse" or "amusing" do you, like me, think that it automatically means "funny" or "humorous?" (And thinking of the church as a place of humor—for some of us that may be a stretch.) Some, on the other hand, are quite amusing but they just don't know it! When I hit that word I thought, "There goes my talk—I am doomed." I couldn't find a scriptural reference talking about being amused in church or in worship. Then I had a thought, what does the word "amuse" actually mean? Here are some synonyms for amuse: to please, gratify, entertain, exhilarate, delight.

I read that list and I thought to myself, hmm . . . sounds an awful lot like what worship ought to be. If we define worship according to the dictionary, it is both a verb and a noun. As a noun, worship is ceremonies, prayers or other religious forms by which love is expressed. As a verb, it is the act of showing love and honor to a deity. So imagine that to amuse God is, in fact, worship. To please Him, to gratify and delight Him. Now delight—there is a very biblical term. I was delighted to find the following passages—or should I say I was amused to find the following passages. Consider:

Psalm 1:1-2: "Blessed is the man who does not walk in the counsel of the wicked or stand in the way of sinners or sit in the seat of mockers. But his delight is in the law of the LORD, and on His law he meditates day and night."

Psalm 35:9: "Then my soul will rejoice in the LORD and delight in His salvation."

Psalm 37:4: "Delight yourself in the LORD and He will give you the desires of your heart."

Psalm 43:4: "Then will I go to the altar of God, to God, my joy and my delight. I will praise You with the harp, O God, my God."

Imagine David, an artist, using his art—song and harp—in worship. Entertaining an audience of one—God!

Psalm 111:2: "Great are the works of the LORD; they are pondered by all who delight in them."

And if you think of this as just an Old Testament thing, consider this reaction by those listening to Jesus after His teaching in the temple courts.

Mark 12:37: " . . . the large crowd listened to Him with delight."

I hope you can see that in this context, being amused can be a godly, biblical thing. Godly and biblical things happening in church would be a good thing, right?

It, of course, can go the other way. Consider:

Psalm 62:4: " . . . they take delight in lies. With their mouths they bless, but in their hearts they curse."

Proverbs 2:14: " . . . who delight in doing wrong and rejoice in the perverseness of evil . . ."

We are not making the word "delight" holy. We are not making the word "entertainment" holy. Like anything, including drama, they can be used for good or evil.

The last word in the definition is "divert." Once again I thought my premise might be in trouble. Especially since some of the sources I used said not only divert, but added "divert attention away from that which is serious." I thought "this is not good, because spiritual things *are* serious." But the more I thought about it, the more I thought "no problem." You see, at least for me, that which I perceive as being serious is more often not the spiritual stuff of life, but rather the "life stuff." In essence, I *need* to divert my attention away from that which really occupies my mind—the serious stuff to do with my work, my family, health, all of life's problems—and instead divert my attention on being entertained, delighted, and amused by the things of God. Now that's entertainment at its best. Entertainment that is directed toward God—be it music, dance, paintings, or drama—that is, or certainly can be, worship.

I realize that when we get down to it, it is not the words as I have defined them but rather the perception of those words . . . it is not the meaning of the word "entertainment" as much as what that word has come to mean in our culture that is at issue here. Steve Pederson, the director of drama at Willow Creek says that is his book *Drama Ministry*:

> The problem for some who oppose the use of drama in the church is the idea that drama is merely entertainment. These people assert that the church should be about the task of saving souls, not about entertainment.
>
> Yes, drama is entertainment, but this fact does not need to be a negative—even in church. Those who object to entertainment in the church usually have a limited definition of it. To them it connotes that which is cheap, glitzy, and worldly—the worst of Las Vegas.
>
> But entertainment can also be truthful and enlightening. Good drama can bring out wholesome laughter or move us deeply. Entertainment for entertainment's sake has no place in church, but entertainment that touches someone's heart and makes that person more open is not only valid, it is desirable.

My assessment is that the church is very much about entertainment, we just don't call it that. The very structure of the sanctuary to the structure of a worship service, whatever your tradition, is designed to hold and focus our attention. While most pastors would reject the label, we all know that the very best preachers are purposeful entertainers. Why else do they tell such good stories and add humor to their message if not to hold our attention and amuse us? Not for entertainment's sake, but so we will listen and receive the message contained within the entertainment.

I want to take this one step further. I think God loves entertainment and loves to be entertained. One need only look at creation and God's repeated delight in what He created. Creating land and water, light and dark, plants and animals, He repeatedly looked and saw that it was good! Read Exodus 35 and 36 to see how God gifted artists, as the scripture says "by His Spirit," to do works of art in building the tabernacle. Read the Psalms and see the enduring art of poet and songwriter David—the man after God's own heart. Look at the theatrics of the Old Testament prophets. I have to think that God was amused and entertained by Elijah. Can you just imagine the great theatre on Mt. Carmel when Elijah called down fire from heaven—what great entertainment!

Drama is about telling a story. Jesus was a master of the parable (defined as a simple story told to illustrate a truth). Isn't that what we are doing when we do drama in worship? The Gospel—the divine drama—is referred to as the greatest story ever told. Art is about entertainment. Few artists create art merely for their own enjoyment, rather they want others to share in the creation. That is true of God—He created man to enjoy and share in His creation. It is true for me when I write a play. My first impulse is to share it with my wife. I want someone else to enjoy my creation. (Sometimes she does.) Art can be for our human entertainment, but it can also be for God's entertainment. When it is, I believe that is an act of worship.

Some might be wondering, "Chuck, are you suggesting that our churches become theatres?" My answer is, "they already are!" Again, going to definitions—theatre is derived from the Greek word *theatron* which means "seeing place." Don't we want the church to be a place where people come to see about God as well as hear about Him? A place that holds our attention? Not, of course, in exclusion to all the other things that take place in the church like fellowship, teaching, and coffee drinking.

"Redeeming" Entertainment

So now the challenge. I want to encourage you to make your entertainment redeeming in its content and value. Not entertainment for entertainment's sake, but rather something that amuses and diverts our attention toward the things of God.

As a Christian artist, I have always had a struggle with the old adage "art for art's sake." The popular notion in the world is that "art needs no defense." "Art just is." I am not saying that there is no room for art that is merely there for no other purpose than our enjoyment, art that "merely entertains." In fact, I think it is possible that even God as an artist made much of creation just because it amused Him with no other purpose in mind. This could be true of the Grand Canyon and it could be true of the duckbilled platypus. It might even be true of some of us here in this room! But as a Christian artist, I think we need to be purposeful in the art we create—maybe not exclusively, but at least in the majority of our time and energy. I say this because I think there is too much at stake not to be purpose driven in our art. If we as Christian artists are not driven with a grander sense of purpose, who then? Certainly there are artists on the other end of the spectrum that are purposeful in their attempts to communicate values and messages most of us would oppose. It is not a secret that we have become an entertainment-oriented culture. We as Christian artists, we as the church, have the challenge of communicating to and reaching that culture. The church needs Christian artists today more than ever. And we need them to spend their energies creating art that will reach this culture. We need Christians at work in theatre that is both overt and subtle. We need them at work in both the church and in the broader culture calling us to the Truth of the Gospel.

I have heard it stated among Christian artists that we do not need to try to get a message across—we should just concentrate on telling a story. That as long as we are Christians producing art, our message will come through who we are. I think this statement may well be a reaction to some of the poorly written and performed plays that have been done in the name of ministry in the past. One of the tendencies we must resist is to simply use our drama to preach rather than to tell a story—which is what drama is supposed to do. The drama we need to be doing should communicate, challenge, foster identification, entertain, and stir us up. It may carry the impact of a sermon, but it should never have preaching as its goal! Leave it to the pastor to preach. To use drama to preach is to risk defeating the greatest strength of drama in the first place—that is, communication without preaching.

But on the other hand, to suggest that redeeming entertainment will just happen without forethought, with no regard to message, bothers me. Oh, this may happen on occasion, but I am troubled by the notion that somehow my work as a writer and as an actor will just happen to have a purposeful value and content simply because I am a Christian. I believe we need to be more intentional than that.

For the last few years I have had the privilege to work with and develop an improv team that now performs a weekly show in Salem. At this time, to the best of my knowledge, all the performers are Christians. We have had some truly great, entertaining moments onstage, but being improv—even at our very best—I would have to say that what we do onstage would appear to be pretty much "entertainment for entertainment's sake." We are Christians performing, but I would hardly call the art we produce of a lasting redeeming quality. There is no "great art" happening here merely because we are Christians. Even though I love what we are doing, if that was the extent of our work in Salem, I think I would come to the conclusion "what a waste." What a waste of time and energy.

You might wonder why we do it if that is all it is? Am I contradicting myself? Didn't I just challenge us all to be more purposeful in the art we create? Yes, I did, but I don't think what we are doing contradicts my challenge and I'll tell you why: I think our culture needs clean, family-friendly entertainment options. Our improvisations may appear to be "merely entertainment," but it is a safe and family-friendly alternative for people to attend. That, in and of itself, is a much-needed ministry. But it is more than that. This venue provides an opportunity for subtle evangelism—people notice that we are different from all the other stuff in town and wonder why. We have the opportunity to tell them. We are providing a place for the Christians in our audience to have a good neutral location to take their friends who may not like or trust the church, a place where they can build relationships that eventually can work their way into a healthy relationship with God and the church. Third, improv is giving me a great vehicle to train actors so that, when we do work on more intentional productions, we will do a better job. And last, while it is yet to happen, I am hopeful that eventually there will be some nonbelieving theatre types that will be attracted to what we are doing—that they will want to join us—and through that process they will come into relationship with Jesus Christ. For these reasons it is no longer "art for art's sake," or "merely entertainment."

For me, redeeming entertainment is entertainment that changes people.

It is the young teenager who sought me out after a performance—not to talk to Chuck Neighbors—but rather to talk with the character I portrayed onstage because she thought that character could help her. You see, this young gal was unmarried and pregnant—the play challenged her and she thought my character could help her. That's redeeming entertainment!

It is the missionary who said to me, "When I came in here tonight I had made up my mind that I was not going back to the mission field—now, after seeing your play, I realize I have to go back." That's redeeming entertainment!

It is the countless number of people who have sat through a one-man comedy and afterward said to me, "I needed that! I needed to laugh!" That is redeeming entertainment.

It is those few times when an entire congregation stands to their feet, not in a standing ovation for the performer, but rather to recommit their lives to following Jesus after—of all things—a one-man play! That is entertainment that redeems! That is the kind of entertainment the church, our society, and our culture need more of.

Being Redeemed as an Entertainer

And as for me, as an artist, I find that I am at my very best when I am about my Master's business. Creating, producing, working, rehearsing, writing, and rewriting all for the sake of the One who created me and wired me to be the unique work of art that I am—that each of us is. When I do this "drama thing" it is an act of worship.

Do you remember the movie *Chariots of Fire*? Some of you are old enough to remember actually seeing it in the theatre. I have always been struck by the scene from *Chariots of Fire* where Eric Liddell is talking to his sister, who wants him not to run in the Olympics but to be a missionary to China. He responds that he has decided to serve as a missionary to China . . . but only after he has run in the Olympics. She is crushed and thinks that he's making the wrong decision. He responds, "God made me to run, and **when I run I feel His pleasure.**"

To feel God's pleasure. Have you ever done something where you felt God's pleasure? I believe that when Eric Liddell ran, he was, in fact, worshiping—doing what God designed him to do. When I perform—not every time, of course, but those times when I am truly in tune, in sync with God when I step onstage—I can truly say that I feel God's pleasure. Like Eric Liddell running the race, I may not always win. Sometimes I merely survive. But then there are those other times when I am "in the zone," I feel the audience, and it is as if we become as one. At those moments I, too, feel His pleasure. That, to me, reflects the heart of Christian artists. A heart of worship, giving our talents and creativity back to the One who gave them to us in the first place. That which holds His attention, and the attention of others. That which diverts attention away from the busy, stressful world that occupies our time and toward our Lord and Savior. That which delights and amuses God and others. He redeems me and He redeems my art. That is entertainment.

So I charge you to go forth and grab attention, amuse, and divert—for the sake of the Kingdom. Go forth and entertain—just be careful where you use the word because to some, it is still the dreaded "E" word.

It's Not Just for Kids

by Chuck Neighbors

First published in "Lillenas Drama Newsletter."

Pet Peeves. Everyone has them, right? Maybe for you it is people who are late for appointments, spouses who don't make the bed, cat hair on your clothing, cold food at McDonald's . . . the list can go on and on.

I lead an exercise called "Fret & Fuss" at my drama workshops. I ask people to find a partner and then share, in animated fashion, one of their pet peeves. The exercise is to help break down inhibitions and also to make observations about how we communicate. Although I have used this exercise many times, I rarely get to participate, as I am leading the group rather than playing along with everyone.

But, I have often thought that I would like a turn at this game. So if you will permit me 60 seconds, I would like to fret and fuss to you about one of my pet peeves. After I finish my rant, I will calm down and explore this frustration more rationally.

Ready? Here goes . . .

Drama is not just for kids! For crying out loud, I am forty . . . something years old, do I look like a kid to you? I hate it when I go to a church and they say something like, "Oh, that's great for the young people." Don't get me wrong—it is great for the young people—but old people like to act too! Think of all the great plays and movies you have ever seen and then go and replace every actor with a high school age student. Give me a break! There would be no Dustin Hoffmans, Meryl Streeps, Paul Newmans, and Katherine Hepburns. People who like to act don't suddenly stop liking to act when they become an adult. It is a gifting, a God-given talent, and done well can have tremendous and life-changing impacts. It is no wonder that Christian drama gets a bad reputation when it is left to "just the kids." I wish the church would elevate the dramatic arts and tap into this powerful medium! We are making progress, but just this week I was on the phone with yet another pastor talking about doing a drama workshop for their church and once again he was stuck in this "great for the young people" box. We don't do that with our music programs—many churches pay big bucks to have the best in Christian music, but when it comes to drama—we get no respect!

OK, take a deep breath. There, I feel better. It is amazing how much better you feel when you take a few minutes to get something that bugs you off your chest.

Now, let's look at this issue more closely. At the heart of the issue is how drama is perceived by a number of adults in the church. The perception by some adults is that drama is childish, unprofessional, and of little substance. It is a good thing for "the kids to do" because it is sometimes "cute," harmless fun, and is an activity that can "keep them out of trouble." It is a great experience that helps the young person develop skills in front of an audience, and we adults love to watch our kids perform. While all these things may be true and even valid reasons for doing drama in church, it comes down to drama being an event that you can invite the grandparents to attend and take some pictures for the family scrapbook.

There's nothing wrong with that! I thank God that I had just those opportunities and have a scrapbook full of cute pictures from my childhood productions. Indeed, I credit those very experiences in helping me discover my passion and calling to theatre today. No question, drama is a good thing for kids!

But contrast that attitude with experiencing a drama that is done on a professional level with material of substance by performers in my own age and peer group. This drama is not a "cute skit," but a play on real life issues that cuts to the heart of the Gospel, leaving audience members in tears or stunned silence. You don't get that kind of quality and impact when drama is left exclusively to the youth of the church. Think back to the plays or movies that you have seen that impacted you, made you cry, or lie awake at night thinking about life. *Schindler's List* comes to mind for me. The scene at the end when Oscar Schindler finally comes to the realization of how many more lives he could have saved was powerful and, for me, theological—I thought about it for days. Drama, done well, can do that to people.

Some of the blame for this "drama is for kids" attitude falls on the shoulders of those who were writing material for the church audience in years gone by. Poor quality material is hard to turn into award-winning drama. And while there is still some pretty poor stuff out there, I am happy to say that there is a lot of good quality material available today! There are quite a number of churches that have discovered the power of good drama done well. The bar has been raised for these churches and the quality of their work shows it.

Do you want to raise the bar for your church? Do you want to see your church perform drama that can change the lives of those in the audience/congregation? If so, here are some practical steps you can take to make it happen:

- **Change your vocabulary.** Don't call the plays "skits" and don't call them "cute." Drama, sketch, play, and vignette are much better alternatives. A skit sounds like something done at camp on talent night—let's leave it there.
- **Cultivate an inner-generational drama team.** Don't exclude the youth, but include the adults. There is no reason to have a 16-year-old play a 60-year-old man if you can get the real thing!
- **Talk up drama with the adults in your church.** Find out who did plays in school, college or community theatre and go after those people.
- **Be on the look-out for talent.** Use social functions at the church as a time to find talented adults to add to the drama team. They are usually easy to spot —they're the ones who make large groups of people laugh or can tell a good story.
- **Get some training.** Take a class on theatre at a community college. Attend a church drama conference (there are several to choose from, call me for de-

tails). Go see plays so you can begin to see the difference between good drama and bad. Hold a drama workshop for the team to teach the basics to all those involved. (You can even book me to do this!)

- **Find good material to perform.** You can start with the books offered by this ministry. Send me an e-mail or give me a call if you want help finding other printed resources.

I am convinced of the power of drama to reach people. I believe that, in light of our current entertainment-oriented culture, it is one of the most effective avenues available to communicate with this world. Let's not use it lightly by leaving it in the hands of children. Let's give it our best for the sake of the Gospel!